T0114938

The Oily Marriage

The Oily Marriage

by

Hope Eghagha

malthouse

Malthouse Press Limited

Lagos, Benin, Ibadan, Jos,Port-Harcourt, Zaria

© Hope Eghagha 2018
First Published 2018
ISBN 978-978-55578-9-3

Malthouse Press Limited
43 Onitana Street, Off Stadium Hotel Road,
Surulere, Lagos, Lagos State
E-mail: malthouse_press@yahoo.com
malthouselagos@gmail.com
Tel: 0802 600 3203

All rights reserved. No part of this publication may be reproduced, transmitted, transcribed, stored in a retrieval system or translated into any language or computer language, in any form or by any means, electronic, mechanical, magnetic, chemical, thermal, manual or otherwise, without the prior consent in writing of Malthouse Press Limited, Lagos, Nigeria.

This book is sold subject to the condition that it shall not by way of trade, or otherwise, be lent, re-sold, hired out, or otherwise circulated without the publisher's prior consent in writing, in any form of binding or cover other than in which it is published and without a similar condition, including this condition, being imposed on the subsequent purchaser.

Distributors:

African Books Collective Ltd
Email: abc@africanbookscollective.com
Website: http://www.africanbookscollective.com

Author's Note

There is something ferociously lusty about the smell of crude oil that attracts both men and women; that makes people want to exploit, decimate or exterminate whole populations of human beings and (or) wildlife; that makes nations and men (gold diggers) kill all obstructing individuals to its acquisition. At the time of writing this play, some indigenous peoples were up in arms against the State in some parts of the world over oil pipes and their danger to the environment. Communities are piling pressure on governments to be more circumspect in the burning drive to extract crude oil from the earth in their God-given natural territories.

It is definitely not for no reason therefore that crude oil is named the 'black gold'; to the typical cigar-smoking, fat-bellied businessman the slick product is a sleeping reservoir of or a guarantee to millions of dollars in the international markets – open and black.

To be sure black gold commands attention both in the open and black markets; the black market is where some slush funds for secret operations are sourced. No questions are asked. No answers are provided. Transparency is not a requirement in the sleazy world of oily operations! The beauty of the 'black gold' is the high road to stupendous wealth which it opens to those who dare; those who sometimes cast aside certain accepted codes of decency and morality to embrace the unwritten unethical rules of survival.

There is also something about the beauty of women that makes some men lose track of the true meaning of a relationship, the true meaning of love and loyalty. There are both archetypal and historical references to the overwhelming power of beauty over the hearts of great men, not-so-great men and ordinary men as well. Solomon in all his wisdom besotted a thousand women, (the recorded ones) I dare say. Pray how many women would the 'wisdomless-man' take? There are times too when a beautiful woman becomes a high stake for men's competition. Sometimes she becomes bait in the power-tussle or scheme of things orchestrated by men. In all recorded history, some women have been used as pawns in the field of intense power play.

When the search for black gold and possession (acquisition is impolite) of beautiful woman become intertwined, we can only imagine how desperate the forces would become. It is true that sometimes the characters involved may not comprehend the level or depth of intrigues at play. Local persons inadvertently become pawns in the hands of powerful persons and interests far away from the source of the commodity.

It is how these persons become inadvertent tools in the hands of the big, wealthy, distant puppeteers that is my major interest in this play. On the road to achieving this objective there are minor themes and issues As a writer whose home region is locked in poverty in spite of abundance of natural wealth, one cannot stay aside and watch. Attention should be drawn to the conflicts and contradictions which ordinary people in exploited societies have to contend with in the daily routine of existence. Whether or not this goal or ambition (?) is dramatically achieved is left for the reading or watching audience to evaluate and pass judgment.

Hope Eghagha
Akoka, Lagos, Nigeria
November 2017

Cast

Cast of *The Oily Marriage* in a premiere production by Art-O-Ten Drama Group on 26 November 2017 in the Arts Theatre of University of Lagos.

Chief Johnson Adjarho – Yomi Ilesanmi
Madam Tiro Adjarho – Stella-Maris Nnaji, Erhieyovwe Obodo
Maiden Adjarho – Temitope Ojubanire, Christiana Ndukwe
Junior Okome – Silas Ezunike Emmanuel Maduka
Alhaji Yusuf- Richard Akinlade, Sixtus Dogman
Bala Yusuf- Emmanuel Maduka, Friday Onyenankeya, Muyiwa Adeosun
Board Secretary – Jessica Godwin, Adenike Ayodele, Christiana Ndukwe
Manager- Chidi Ihejewu, Oluwaseyi Omoyele
Public Relations Officer - Bernard Sunday Victor, Anie Adolf Umoh, Kingsley Ahuekwe, Oluseyi Omoyele
Dr. Odion Alebai – Odilanme Eze, Adeshina Ismaila,
Mrs. Abigo Alebai- Erhieyovwe, Stella-Maris Nnaji, Janet Aboyeji
Miss Gberaja Suru – Adenike Ayodele, Ngozi Udenna, Eunice Emmanuel
Chief Odidi Koloko- Sixtus Dogman, Friday Onyenankeya, Oluwaseyi Omoyele
Youth Leader 'Omimi' – Alimison Babajide, Sadiya Omololu, Goddey Johnson,

Youth of the Community- Goddey Johnson, Oluwaseyi
  Omoyele, Christiana Ndukwe, Chidi Ihejewuru,
  Nike Idika, Ngozi Udenna, Omololu Omoyele,
  George Eyo, Friday Onyenankeya, Jessica
  Godwin, Odilanme Eze, Adeshina Ismaila,
  Eunice Emmanuel.

Politician (Chief Awoko) – Sadiya Omololu, Oluwaseyi
  Omoyele, Friday Onyenankeya, Olasunkanmi
  Daramola

Madam Owhawha – Ngozi Udenna, Jenet Aboyeji

Ms. Stella Oshare- Adenike Ayodele, Nike Idika, Eunice
  Emmanuel

Bishop- George Eyo, Bernard Sunday Victor, Anie Adolf
  Umoh

Benson – Kingsley Ahuekwe, Oluwaseyi Omoyele, Anie
  Adolf Umoh

Production Crew

Director- Art Osagie Okedigun
Visiting Director- William Benson
Assistant Director- Muyiwa Adeosun
Stage Manager- Matthew Oluwatobi
Assistant Stage Manager- Goddey Johnson
Production Manager- Olasunkanmi Daramola
Production Assistants – Odilanme Eze, Anie Adolf Umoh,
Welfare- Ngozi Udenna, Elizabeth Fagbeyiro
Costumes- Goddey Johnson
Costumes Designer- Art Osagie Okedigun
Make-up- Manager- Nike Idika
Make-up Artist- Adenike Ayodele
Props Management Team- George Eyo, Babajide
  Alimison
Light Designer- Femi Adeniyi
Light Assistant- Olasunkanmi Daramola

Sound and Drummers- D.J. AK, Taiwo K. Adesoji,
Mayowa Olayiwola, Alfred Babatunde Idris,
Muyiwa Adefila
Choreographer- Emeka A. Okolie
Technical Director- Olasunkanmi Daramola
Stage Designer- Art Osagie Okedigun, Olasunkanmi
Daramola, Femi Adeniyi, Goddey Johnson
Documentation – Muyiwa Adeosun (Photography)
Human Relations Officer – Temitope Ojubanire
Graphic Designer- Eunice Emmanuel
Online Media & Publicity – Exkayz Productions, Inside
Art Productions

The Oily Marriage

Characters

Chief Johnson Adjarho
Madam Tiro Adjarho
Maiden Adjarho
Junior, Okome & Voke – sons of Chief Adjarho
Alhaji Yusuf
Mr. Bala Yusuf
Board Secretary
Manager
Public Relations Officer
Dr. Odion Alebai – University lecturer
Mrs. Abigo Alebai – mother to Odion
Miss Gberaja Suru
Chief Odidi Koloko
Youth Leader – Omimi alias *Broke the Bottle*
Youths of the Community
Politician – Chief Awoko
Madam Owhawha – political stalwart
Ms. Stella Oshare - political stalwart
Bishop
Benson - Houseboy

Act One

Scene One

(Chief Adjarho's house. It is well furnished with modern furniture, pictures of State officials and other paraphernalia; as a Community Leader, he is affluent and influential. It shows in the quality of the furniture, his dressing and his carriage).

Chief Adjarho: *(Sarcastically)* Is there going to be a life-changing party this afternoon?

Tiro: Life-changing party! I don't know where you pick up such grand expressions from!

Chief Adjarho: Give it to the man who is always reading books!

Tiro: Well, I'm not planning any party. But why do you ask?

Chief Adjarho: You two, mother and daughter are behaving funny?

Maiden: Daddy!

Tiro: Behaving funny? How do you mean?

Chief Adjarho: I smell something in the air!

Maiden: Daddy always smells things anyway!

Tiro: Something like the scent of food?

Chief Adjarho: Naah!

Tiro: Like the smell of oil money? I know you love that!

Chief Adjarho: Yes I love the smell of oil money. Is there anything wrong with that?

Tiro: No, nothing wrong with loving the smell of oil-money which is under the soil of your house!

Chief Adjarho: Good. I sense something positively dramatic is about to happen!

Tiro: You do? What gives you that feeling?

Chief Adjarho: You have put on one your best attires…

Tiro: Means nothing. I believe that a woman should always look spick and span, whether at home or in the office or wherever!

Chief Adjarho: And you Maiden, your eyes have not left the window since you came into the sitting room, darting here and there.

Junior: May be mom and her precious daughter are expecting the Governor!

Maiden: Governor indeed!

Chief Adjarho: Whatever…!

Tiro: No, it's the President of the country we are expecting!

Junior: Or have you got yourself a fiancée?

Chief Adjarho: That would be good news. I need to celebrate my daughter. For too long have I been attending wedding ceremonies of other families; I need to bomb the town with a party of who-is-who in the State!

Tiro: Hmmmm! Bomb the town…!

Chief Adjarho: For a change, let the celebration come from my house!

Junior: And we shall provide enough drinks and food for the community for weeks! My only sister's wedding? It will be the bomb!

Chief Adjarho: Yes, my son.

Junior: I will dance *azonto* all night!

Maiden: Not only *azonto*; you will dance *shoki* too!

Tiro: And *shakiti bobo*!

Junior: When is the big day?

Chief Adjarho: Junior, you are dreaming about your sister's wedding!

Junior: Yes daddy…

Chief Adjarho: Who says you should not get married too?

Junior: Daddy!

Chief Adjarho: You think I don't want another daughter in the house?

Junior: When I get a good job to stabilize me, I will get married.

Chief Adjarho: If I waited to have everything before marriage you wouldn't have come into the world!

Junior: Your time was different daddy.

Chief Adjarho: Different how?

Junior: The cost of renting a flat frightens me. If only I would get a good job from one of the companies in this town!

Chief Adjarho: I'm working on that…

Junior: Instead of employing us they bring people from other parts of the country!

Tiro: Tragic, very exploitative!

Junior: They then deceive and impregnate our girls and disappear.

Chief Adjarho: That will stop soon. We are preparing a Memorandum of Understanding that will change all of that. The Federal Government has been sluggish because of powerful forces working against us. But with the agitation by our youth, they are beginning to listen.

Junior: Why should they wait for violent agitation to listen to us?

Chief Adjarho: I don't know…

Tiro: It's the way of the world; in all history the powerful have always exploited the weak. Except you fight for your rights you nobody will grant them. Nigeria fought the British to gain Independence. What about Blacks in America? How did apartheid come to an end in South

Africa? Fight. Liberation struggle! That's the language the oppressor understands. So we in the Niger Delta have to fight to control our God-given resource!

Chief Adjarho: Yes, fight for justice. See the way they have pushed our boys into bombing oil facilities and all kinds of atrocities?

Tiro: Including kidnapping for money! Criminals now use the struggle as subterfuge to do terrible things!

Chief Adjarho: Well, today, I am concerned with the struggle inside my family. Just bring me a good beautiful girl that you want to marry. Okay? I want my grand children around me.

Junior: Who says I won't like to marry, live a comfortable life with my wife and kids?

Chief Adjarho: Okay oo. Just continue to wait for the ideal time; just make sure you don't become an old man before you take a wife.

Junior: My plans are in the pipeline!

Chief Adjarho: Don't let them remain in the pipeline forever. The time is now!

Tiro: The time is now, I like that. The time for action is now!

Chief Adjarho: Yes...

Tiro: Your daughter has risen to the occasion!

Chief Adjarho: Really?

Tiro: Yes; you have always said that our daughter should bring her man to the house…

Chief Adjarho: Yes. Is he coming today? Maiden, is your man coming today?

Maiden: *(Shyly)* Yes dad!

Chief Adjarho: Good. I said it. I have become a prophet, yet no one would honour me in the family. Where is he coming from?

Maiden: He came in from Lagos yesterday evening.

Chief Adjarho: So, he is in town already? I see. A long distance…Was that where you met him? Lagos?

Maiden: Yes daddy.

Chief Adjarho: So while I was paying your school fees you were busy looking for a man in the university!

Tiro: Johnson! How could you say that?

Maiden: Daddy!

Chief Adjarho: I was only pulling your legs! You are a beautiful girl and men would naturally look for you the way I plucked your nubile and beautiful mother from her father's tree! *(Roars into laughter)*

Tiro: I don't know whether to laugh or just ignore you!

Chief Adjarho: Do your best…What have you prepared for him? I hope there are drinks in the fridge!

Tiro: There are drinks. And there is food too.

Chief Adjarho: Junior, make sure there are drinks in the fridge

Junior: Yes dad…there are enough drinks.

Chief Adjarho: I hope the young man knows what to do when he visits his future father-in-law!

Tiro: Daddy, but this is just to know you, and for you to ask about his family background and to know him too.

Chief Adjarho: Our people say '*ebe evwre mu oyen eruemu*', things must be done properly.

Tiro: But he is not from this town, he is not an Urhobo man!

Chief Adjarho: Madam Lawyer! *(Bellowing)* Benson!

(Benson dashes into the sitting room)

Chief Adjarho: Get the usual things ready for our visitors!

Benson: What sir?

Chief Adjarho: Bone head! Get some kola nuts ready and a bottle of schnapps!

Benson: Yes Sir.

Chief Adjarho: Must I repeat everything to you?

Tiro: Daaddy! He barely understood you. Did you think he would read your mind and immediately understand what you wanted?

Chief Adjarho: When you carry the tree of life on your head, remember not to greet the dead on the way.

Tiro: I just wonder how you changed to be so traditional in the space of five years!

Chief Adjarho: Changed?

Tiro: Yes, you have changed. You were not like this in our days in Lagos.

Chief Adjarho: I have always been like this. There was no need to be traditional in a place where everybody was forming *oyibo*! They would have called me a bush man! **(Bursts into loud laughter)** And you Bone head, what are you still doing here? Vanish!

(Benson practically vanishes)

Chief Adjarho: While we were in Lagos didn't you see potential sons-in-law prostrate themselves before their parents-in-law? Didn't their men wear *agbada* to the office? But because we were foreigners there we couldn't do traditional things. Our elders say that when a lame woman hears good music she dances with her heart. Now that I am home, the king must be honoured in his land!

Tiro: It must be a lame woman! Not a lame man!

Chief Adjarho: Okay…a feminist manifesto camp is brewing..when a lame person! Are you satisfied?

Tiro: I agree with you to an extent…

Chief Adjarho: I am satisfied that you agree with me to some extent. Let the boy comply!

Tiro: It's not a formal thing he is coming for; please don't bully him when he comes…

Chief Adjarho: Woman, am I a bully?

Tiro: You are not a bully, though sometimes you bully people.

(Knock on the door)

Tiro: Maiden, please find out who is at the door! It may be your friend.

Maiden: Yes mom. *(She goes to open the door. Smile on her face)* Welcome to my home! *(Alebai enters)*

Dr. Alebai: Thanks. *(Kneeling down)* Good afternoon Sir. *Migwo* Sir! *Migwo* ma!

Chief Adjarho: Vre. How are you? *(Alebai stands up)*

Dr. Alebai: I'm fine Sir. Thank you. How are you Sir?

Chief Adjarho: We are great.

Dr. Alebai: Thank God Sir.

Chief Adjarho: Who are you, young man?

Dr. Alebai: I am…

Tiro: He is Maiden's visitor I told you about.

Chief Adjarho: You are very welcome. Please sit down.
    Excuse me…Benson!

(Maiden slips out of the sitting room)

Voice: Sir, I'm coming with the drinks and kola.

Chief Adjarho: Better. So young man, I'm told you came
    into town yesterday.

Dr. Alebai: Yes Sir.

Chief Adjarho: You are welcome to the Delta, the home of
    hospitality and friendship. **(Drinks arrive)** We shall
    give you a special treat Niger Delta fashion.

Dr. Alebai: I'm grateful sir.

Chief Adjarho: Junior!

Junior: Yes daddy. *(He stands up to do the formal
    presentation) Migwo!*

Chief Adjarho: *Vre do*

Junior: *Adjerese!*

Chief Adjarho: *Oyen ese!*

Junior: Our dear visitor, what's your praise name?

Dr. Alebai: I don't have any!

Junior: *I-Don't-Have-Any*, my father says I should welcome
    you on his behalf. Here are drinks and kola nut.

Dr. Alebai: Thank you Sir. *Migwo*

Junior: In our tradition the kola has to be wedged with money so it does not fall to the ground. Here is money, the sum of five thousand naira to support the kola. All of these are for you.

Dr. Alebai: Thank you Sir.

(Tiro offers some money to Junior)

Junior: My mother supports the kola with the sum of two thousand naira.

Dr. Alebai: Thank you sir. *Migwo* ma

Junior: I'm not like the *agbero*, the motor park tout who gives seats to passengers and treks home; so, I'm also supporting my father with the sum of one thousand naira! All these are for you. The drinks we will drink together; the kola nut we will also share. The money is for you. That's the message my father sent me. *Siagware*!

All: *Iya!*

Dr. Alebai: I'm grateful Sir. All of these are for me? I'm deeply moved. God bless you sir.

Chief: Junior, receive the drinks on his behalf!

Junior: *Adjerese!*

Chief Adjarho: *Onye ese!*

Junior: *I-Don't-Have-Any* says he is happy that you have received him; that when he entered the house, the smile on your face was more than food and drinks. That he didn't expect to receive such huge sums of money. That he is grateful to keep the money and that we should all share the drinks and eat the kola nuts. *Sia gware*!

All: *Iya!*

(Junior takes the drink to Chief Adjarho who prays in the traditional way. The kola nut is shared. While eating and drinking Chief wastes no time)

Chief Adjarho: Young man, this prayer is for you. *(He kneels down)* May you travel well, travel safely, travel when the road is not hungry.

Dr. Alebai: *Ise!*

Chief Adjarho: May your father eat the fruit of your labour; and your mother too!

Dr. Alebai: It is life we pray for; may we enjoy the life in good health and long life.

Chief Adjarho: The frog leaps forward only; may you leap forward like the frog.

Dr. Alebai: *Ise!*

Chief Adjarho: The elephant does not look back. Life will never look back on you.

Dr. Alebai: Ise!

Chief Adjarho: The water meant for you will get to your tongue.

Dr. Alebai: *Ise!*

Chief Adjarho: It will not choke you!

Dr. Alebai: *Ise!*

Chief Adjarho: I pray for you my wife; God will bless you.

Tiro: *Ise!*

Chief Adjarho: You are a mother of children; may you be a mother of many grandchildren!

Tiro: *Ise!*

Chief Adjarho: You will live long!

Tiro: *Ise!*

Chief Adjarho: Longer than your mother and grandmother!

Tiro: *Ise!*

Chief Adjarho: I pray for you Junior. May God bless you!

Junior: *Ise!*

Chief Adjarho: With a good job!

Junior: *Ise!*

Chief Adjarho: With a good life!

Junior: *Ise!*

Chief Adjarho: You will live long!

Junior: *Ise!*

Chief Adjarho: You are like a tree; anyone who tries to shake you can only shake his head!

Junior: *Ise!*

Chief Adjarho: The prayer covers me too. What I have worked for with my hands, my mouth will eat it!

All: *Ise!*

Chief Adjarho: *Siagware!*

All: *Iya!*

(They share the drinks and eat kola nuts.)

Chief Adjarho: Young man, let me know you properly. Where is your home town?

Dr. Alebai: I'm an Edo man from Uzebba. My late father was Engr. Odion Alebai. He…

Chief Adjarho: Odion Alebai?

Dr. Alebai: Yes Sir!

Chief Adjarho: Did he work at Lagos textile Mills in Oshodi?

Dr. Alebai: Yes Sir!

Chief Adjarho: What a small world! Is your mother's name Abigo?

Dr. Alebai: Yes Sir, that's my mother's name.

Chief Adjarho: Hmmm *(Pensive)*

Tiro: Is anything the matter?

(Silence)

Tiro: Johnson, what's the matter?

Chief Adjarho: Nothing. I knew his parents long ago.
Where is your dad?

Dr. Alebai: Unfortunately he died about five years ago.

Chief Adjarho: And your mother?

Dr. Alebai: She's retired now; she runs a maternity clinic in
Benin.

Chief Adjarho: I see. Did you tell her you were coming to
see me?

Dr. Alebai: I didn't mention your name. I just told her I was
going to see Maiden's family in Warri!

Chief Adjarho: Okay. *(Chief's mood has changed; he is not
the jocular fellow who started the scene)* You are welcome
my son.

Dr. Alebai: Thank you Sir.

Chief Adjarho: What do you do for a living?

Dr. Alebai: I'm a lecturer in the university.

Chief Adjarho: Good. I hear they don't pay you teachers
very well.

Dr. Alebai: Things certainly can be better.

Tiro: It's better than it used to be ten years ago.

Chief Adjarho: Tell me more about the university. How come our universities cannot compete with their counterparts abroad?

Dr. Alebai: It's due to poor funding, lack of infrastructure, poor working conditions. Often the universities carry on without constant power supply and research facilities.

Chief Adjarho: Power supply? That should be easy! Why can't your Engineering Faculty develop the infrastructure that will give you people light?

Dr. Alebai: It's a complex matter...

Chief Adjarho: What is complex? I once visited an Engineering Faculty in which there was no power in the Dean's office. I asked the professor why he couldn't ask his students to fabricate a device that could store solar energy. He gave me a foolish answer. I didn't tell him that though; it was when I was looking for admission for my son. I had to talk nicely. If a Department of Electrical Engineering cannot fabricate simple equipment that could trap energy from the sun, they should close shop.

Dr. Alebai: You have a point there sir. But you see...

Tiro: It is the national malaise that is affecting our universities. See what we are doing with our oil! No investments; once the price of oil in the international market falls, it is trouble for the country. Our oil will not last forever; so we have to make hay while the sun shines!

Chief Adjarho: *(His mobile phone rings)* Yes? ...Chief Adjarho speaking... No... are you sure? When did they start the plan?...I'm surprised that it's just getting to me. It's okay. I will deal with the situation tomorrow. No, they are yet to respond. I hope they do soon... if they don't, let's cross the bridge when we get there. Okay. Bye! *(End of call)* So young man, you say you want to marry my daughter?

Tiro: He has merely come to present himself...

Chief Adjarho: My son, you want to marry my daughter?

Dr. Alebai: Yes Sir!

Chief Adjarho: And you walked here to my house all the way from Lagos naked? All by yourself? Is that how you marry a girl in your place?

Dr. Alebai: I'm sorry Sir. I just came to know you.

Chief Adjarho: This is the problem with our youth. They do not know culture; yet they won't ask to be taught. Marriage, my son, is a sacred thing. It is the union of two families. At no time in the process should a groom-to-be move alone. Do you hear me?

Dr. Alebai: Yes sir!

Tiro: He is sorry daddy.

Chief Adjarho: In Urhobo culture, whenever you go on a visit to your potential in-laws you must go with a bottle of hot drink, kola nuts and some money to support the kola. It is a way of showing how serious you are; it also shows respect for tradition. Okay?

Dr. Alebai: Okay sir. Thank you Sir!

Junior: He is sorry. He won't do that next time!

Tiro: He has learnt his lesson!

Chief Adjarho: It's okay. You are welcome. I'm expecting some friends. Tiro, entertain him in the other living room before my friends arrive.

(Knock. While Tiro leads Alebai off the stage Junior gets the door. Koloko enters)

Chief Adjarho: My brother, welcome to my humble abode!

Koloko: Humble? This is a fantastic edifice. How have you been?

Chief Adjarho: I thank God. I've been very fine. We can't complain. How are you?

Koloko: I'm very fine. The boys are at it again.

Chief Adjarho: Which boys?

Koloko: The community boys are planning a protest tomorrow. I thought I should let you know before time.

Chief Adjarho: What's their grievance? The usual stuff?

Koloko: No; this time they want to be given the job of securing the pipelines which run through the community.

Chief Adjarho: They have my support. Is it not an insult to import young men from across the Niger to come into our towns and villages to guard pipelines?

Koloko: The federal authorities won't listen. The boys want to target Yusuf. He is a symbol of all they are angry about.

Chief Adjarho: It's okay; thanks for the information. I will be ready for them. I will send the usual message so that some funds can be made available for me to demobilize them after the protest.

Koloko: Remember me when you receive demobilization o!

Chief Adjarho: Of course. You are a dependable ally and you need encouragement.

Koloko: *(Bringing out some drinks, money and kola nut from his bag)* My daughter will get married on the 16th of next month. I'm using these items to invite you.

Chief Adjarho: Congratulations. May God bless the union!

Koloko: Amen!

Chief Adjarho: I accept the drinks and kola! We shall be there in full force!

Koloko: *Migwo*!

Chief Koloko: *Vre do*! Which of your daughters?

Koloko: The second one, Rugba. You know that my first girl Yoreme has been very foolish.

Chief Adjarho: She will come to her senses someday.

Koloko: I hope it won't be too late then.

Chief Adjarho: Who is the lucky man?

Koloko: It's Chief Ogbogbo's first son, the one who just returned from America.

Chief Adjarho: You see! That's what should be happening here. Let our girls marry our boys.

Koloko: That's the best thing to happen; however, if any man, even from the moon comes for Yoreme my daughter I will gladly arrange the marriage and send her away. I will foot the bill one hundred percent.

Chief Adjarho: That I will understand. She has remained for too long and she has to marry before she *kwe ki*! But a young vibrant beautiful girl should marry around here; marry one of our boys.

Koloko: I agree. *(Conspiratorially)* I hear Yusuf wants to arrange your daughter for his son?

Chief Adjarho: Yusuf? Nobody has told me!

Koloko: You know I have my ears to the ground.

Chief Adjarho: How can he be talking about marrying my daughter without telling me first? Is he taking me for-granted?

Koloko: Well, I do not think so. I believe he will come to you soon. The information got to me because I am paid to know what is going on in the community.

Chief Adjarho: I trust you. Well, I won't say anything yet. Our elders say that a man doesn't show undue haste when he is going to where we will stay the night.

(Tiro, Maiden and Dr. Alebai come in from inside the room)

Tiro: Chief Koloko! *Migwo!*

Koloko: *Vre do.* How are you?

Tiro: We are doing great. How's madam?

Koloko: She is well.

Chief Adjarho: Chief Koloko has brought us an invitation; his daughter is getting married to Chief Ogbogbo's son next month.

Tiro: That is good news. Congratulations.

Koloko: Who is this handsome young man who resembles you so much chief?

Tiro: He is Maiden's friend who is visiting with us. Come to think about it, Dr. Alebai resembles you

Chief Adjarho: Really? That is interesting. It has been said that all of us have about eight look-alikes in the world. How true it is I don't know.

Koloko: How are you young man?

Dr. Alebai: I am fine. *Migwo* sir.

Koloko: *Vre* do

Dr. Alebai: Good to meet you Sir. How are you?

Koloko: I am great. How long will you be here?

Tiro: He has to leave now to be able to catch his flight to Lagos.

Chief Adjarho: Good.

Koloko: If he is not mobile I will give him a ride to the airport.

Tiro: That's kind of you. But Junior and Maiden will take him to the airport.

Alebai: Thank you Sir.

Chief Adjarho: Have a safe trip.

Dr. Alebai: Thank you Sir.

(They all move to the door. Koloko, Dr. Alebai, Junior and Maiden leave. Chief Adjarho and Tiro return to the sitting room)

Chief Adjarho: Tell Maiden that she hasn't found a husband yet.

Tiro: Why? What is the matter?

Chief Adjarho: I will explain some other time; but for now, accept my decision like a good wife.

Tiro: What explanation are we going to give to Maiden? She will feel very bad.

Chief Adjarho: It's not all times that we must explain things, particularly to our children. Sometimes they should trust our judgment as parents.

Tiro: Trust your judgment you mean. I do not see any reason why they should not be given a chance.

Chief Adjarho: I am going for a meeting at the Local Government secretariat.

Tiro: See how you have abruptly changed the subject.

Chief Adjarho: Benson!

Tiro: Johnson!

(Benson rushes in)

Chief Adjarho: Tell the driver to bring my car to the front house!

Benson: Yes sir!

(Tiro is shaking her head)

(Sharp lights out)

Scene Two

(A peaceful demonstration buoyed by chanting is in progress. Youths, boys and girls carry placards in protest against oppression, unemployment, non-indigenes getting all the juicy jobs. It is the typical youth protest, with hoodlums often joining and making all kinds of scenes)

"All we are saying give us our jobs".

"All we are saying give us our jobs"

"All we are saying more jobs for us"

"All we are saying don't take our oil"

(They use the auditorium and end up in the compound of Chief Adjarho. The leader Omimi alias "Broke the Bottle" addresses the audience.)

Youth One: Enough is enough!

Youth Two: Our leaders must listen to us!

Female Youth One: Monkey dey work baboon dey chop! Empowerment for the girls!

Youth One: Empowerment for the youths!

Female Youth Two: Employment for all the youths in the oil-bearing towns and communities!

Youth Two: We don tire for promise and fail!

Omimi: Everyday they tell us not to worry, to be peaceful.

Youth One: Broke the Bottle!

Omimi: Na me be dat!

Youth Two: Scatter the Bottle

Omimi: Na my name be that!

(Chief Adjarho comes out. They hail him, and the noise subsides.)

Youth One: Silence! Let's keep quiet and hear our leader!

All: Silence! Silence!

Omimi: Leader, we greet you.

Chief Adjarho: I greet you all my brothers and sisters!

Omimi: We have come to let you know our grievances. It's not that you do not know them. You know them very well. But the situation is getting worse, worse and worse.

Youth Two: Even worser sef!

Female Youth: No be only worser, na worsest!

Omimi: The oil in our land will not last forever. All the jobs from the oil prospecting firms are given to foreigners, people who are not Nigerians and Nigerians from other states. Even the small jobs which we can use to eat are given to non-indigenes. This is not right. This must stop. See the contractors doing all the jobs. Can't some be given to our men and women? Who says we cannot do contract? We are giving **FLAMES OIL COMPANY (FOC)** a ten-day ultimatum; except they recruit our boys or give jobs to our people, we will turn the town upside down. All the other companies like the one owned by Alhaji Yusuf in the town must give jobs to our boys.

Female Youth: Break the Bottle!

Omimi: Na me be dat!

Female Youth: I say scatter the Bottle!

Omimi: Na me ooo na me be dat! Tell the government that all oil companies should bring their headquarters to the region. Do they think we do not like beautiful houses or beautiful offices? See those fine houses in the federal capital; we want them here as well. We need bridges like the long Third Mainland Bridge in the former federal capital. We are not for violence. We preach against violence. People who use violence often lose their own property. We are for peace. But nobody should take us for-granted any more.

Youth One: We no go gree o we no go gree. Niger Delta we no go gree! *(They break into a song.)*

Chief Adjarho: Up youths!

All: Action!

Chief Adjarho: Up up youths!

All: Action!

Chief Adjarho: My dear youths! Let me tell you that I feel what you feel. The situation in our land is tragic. I agree with you that you should be given jobs. I also agree that our contractors should get contracts and do supplies. The claim that our people lack the expertise is not true. In my house, I have graduate sons who are not employed. Instead FOC usually gets notes from big men in the capital and employ their children here. I support your protest.

Youth Two: Fire on!

Chief Adjarho: However, we are fighting the big issue. We want to control our resources. We are asking for true federalism. When and if we practice true federalism, we will control our oil and employment will not be a problem. Our national leader has submitted a paper to the Federal Government which asks for true federalism. Some day we shall march on the Federal Capital which was built with funds from the oil sucked out of our earth.

Youths: Yes!

The thieves!

Iji!

Chief Adjarho: Freedom will come to our land. And for
   that day we all must labour; unlike the animals in *Animal
   Farm*, we shall not die before freedom comes!

Youths: We shall not die!

   We must eat the fruit of our land!

Omimi: *So gwe!*

All: Eh!

Omimi: *So gwe!*

All: *Iya!*

Omimi: We have presented our demands to our Community
   leader; let us now march to the office of FLAMES in the
   other part of town

(They break into a song)

   Solidarity forever

   Solidarity forever

   Solidarity forever

   We must always fight for our rights!

   ***(They leave the stage. Chief Adjarho enters his
   sitting room)***

Chief Adjarho: Please give me a bottle of water!

Tiro: Benson!

Voice: Ma!

Tiro: Get daddy a bottle of water

Voice: Yes ma!

(Benson enters with a tray and a bottle of water. Serves Chief Adjarho)

Chief Adjarho: It's never easy to handle such a crowd. Thank God that these young men are friendly and sensible. If they turn against you? *Hehehehehe!*

Tiro: That's why as leaders we must always be on the side of the people.

Chief Adjarho: Easier said…

Tiro: Why?

(Knock on the door. Alhaji Yusuf enters)

Chief Adjarho: Alhaji himself!

Alhaji Yusuf: It's good to meet you at home Chief!

Chief Adjarho: You are welcome. How are you? How is your family?

Alhaji Yusuf: Everything is alright, though things could be better. There is fire on the mountain!

Tiro: Good afternoon Sir!

Yusuf: Madam, good afternoon. How are your children?

Tiro: They are fine. Thank you. I guess I must excuse myself so both of you can talk freely.

Chief Adjarho: Please ask Benson to get a bottle of malt drink for Mr. Yusuf.

Tiro: I will

Chief Adjarho: It's rare to see you around here this time. To what do I owe this honour?

Alhaji Yusuf: It's good to visit you. After all you are the community leader. I must pay my homage! In fact, there is fire on the mountain!

(Benson enters with drinks. Serves Alhaji Yusuf)

Alhaji Yusuf: I heard that the youths demonstrated today.

Chief Adjarho: O yes. They left my place a few minutes ago.

Alhaji Yusuf: What's their problem this time?

Chief Adjarho: The usual complaints; how non-indigenes like Yusuf have hijacked the oil business from sons of the soil.

Alhaji Yusuf: We are all one Chief, aren't we?

Chief Adjarho: Yes we are all one as people of the same country. But the real power is in the hands of a few.

Alhaji Yusuf: Chief! What do you mean? Aren't you one of the power holders in this land?

Chief Adjarho: Yusuf, I cannot be deceived. Let's not deceive ourselves. The real power in this country is in the hands of a few people. Do you think if this oil in our land were located in your place your people would allow me to build a house, settle in your community and call the shots in the award of contracts?

Alhaji Yusuf: It is not like that Chief!

Chief Adjarho: It is like that my Alhaji! But the tide is changing. Our boys have become restless. They have seen all the beautiful buildings and things in the federal capital. They want the resources of the land put to use here too. As a leader I advocate peace; we have seen war before. It didn't help anybody. I'm not in support of those boys who have been bombing facilities. The truth however is that if you do not listen to us the peace makers, we will not be able to control the violent ones.

Alhaji Yusuf: I have always maintained that we are one. That is why you people have accommodated me here. Of course we too would have accommodated you in our place. Blowing up pipes affects oil production and the revenue that comes to your people. I live here; I feel sorry for the people. By the way, there is something I want to mention to you in confidence. (**Lowers his voice)** Please teach me how to go about it. I want to arrange the marriage.

Chief Adjarho: This is a delicate matter.

Alhaji Yusuf: I'm just preparing your mind. I know what to
    do.

Chief Adjarho: I have heard you with one ear!

Alhaji Yusuf: I have said things from one corner of my
    mouth.

Chief Adjarho: Good. If you ask people in town, they will
    tell you how to walk the road of marriage.

Alhaji Yusuf: I know. I will do the right thing.

Chief Adjarho: Let me ask you a question. Does your son
    know my daughter?

Alhaji Yusuf: I think so. You know these things….

Chief Adjarho: It's okay. We shall see how things go.

Alhaji Yusuf: I have to leave now. *(Standing up and
    moving to the door)* Please handle the boys so that
    their protests do not get out of hand. *(Drops a parcel)*
    Please I leave this as welfare funds for you and the boys.

Chief Adjarho: Thank you; I am sure you know things
    work here. *(He quickly tucks the envelop into a
    drawer)*

Alhaji Yusuf: I do; just use a little to wipe your own nose
    too!

Chief Adjarho: Trust me; but certain things must be done
    to change the plight of our people.

Alhaji Yusuf: Yes I agree with you.

(He leaves. As Chief Adjarho gets to his seat, Tiro reappears)

Tiro: I can see that your friend has gone!

Chief Adjarho: Yes

Tiro: Good riddance

Chief Adjarho: I know you have never liked the man

Tiro: I don't like his ways!

Chief Adjarho: Why?

Tiro: His ways are very oily, crooked!

Chief Adjarho: Don't judge him too harshly. I guess if we were in his shoes we would do the same.

Tiro: Do the same? How?

Chief Adjarho: Exploit every opportunity offered by the comfort of our ethnic group…

Tito: You have become his advocate…

Chief Adjarho: Well, I have always been fair dealing with people…

Tiro: Have they been fair in their dealings with you?

Chief Adjarho: I leave that to posterity. Yusuf is a businessman and you must understand him from that perspective. My relationship with him has helped a great deal

Tiro: I know; the opposite ought to be the case!

Chief Adjarho: Well...

Tiro: What brought him here today?

Chief Adjarho: He says that he came to greet me. But before he left, he whispered something into my ear.

Tiro: What was it?

Chief Adjarho: He said his son is interested in my daughter!

Tiro: Which daughter?

Chief Adjarho: Which daughter? How many daughters do I have?

Tiro: Do I know? I hope it is not our daughter!

Chief Adjarho: Listen woman let us discuss this matter dispassionately.

Tiro: I hope you didn't give any response

Chief Adjarho: Trust me. I'm not a child of yesterday!

Tiro: What did you tell him?

Chief Adjarho: That I have heard with only one ear!

Tiro: Me oo! I have not heard it at all. Does his son know Maiden?

Chief Adjarho: That's the same question I asked him

Tiro: He has not spoken to Maiden; they have not really met. But he wants to marry her!

Chief Adjarho: If things were normal it won't be bad for two families to arrange a marriage. It works sometimes.

Tiro: Not in the 21st century!

Chief Adjarho: Let's not go into that. There have been many arranged marriages which turned out to be successful.

Tiro: Well, my daughter has a fiancée already

Chief Adjarho: My daughter does not have a fiancée yet!

Tiro: Hmmmmm! I suppose at some point we would need to ask the person in the centre of it all what her opinion is!

Chief Adjarho: Sure. But wait a minute! Why don't we just dream?

Tiro: Dream? How?

Chief Adjarho: Can you imagine the wedding we would host in this town? Even the President of the Federal Republic will be present; of course the Governor of the State will be there too, along with other governors and

Senators and elected officials. You know what that would do for me?

Tiro: That's your dream; not mine! My daughter will marry the man she loves; she will not be used as part of the exchange in a business transaction!

Chief Adjarho: At the national level, I' be recognized. Big jobs would follow and the sky would be our limit!

Tiro: Count me out!

Chief Adjarho: I could even become a Minister of the Federal Republic!

Tiro: That's the problem with our people! They like crumbs; they like to be fed with crumbs from the master's table. Have you thought about your daughter's happiness? Have you thought about the happiness of your people? Only a few moments ago the youths were here and you told them that you were fighting for true federalism for them. Is this part of it? To give out your daughter in order to climb the social ladder and collect a brown envelop?

Chief Adjarho: As Minister of Works, all the roads in our region will be tarred.

Tiro: Wake up Chief Adjarho!

Chief Adjarho: I will sit in Council with the President of the country dressed in our traditional attire, hat beads and all!

Tiro: Maiden! Maiden!

Chief Adjarho: Guarded by policemen and driven around in a Lexus SUV?

Voice: Yes mom! *(She enters)*

Chief Adjarho: Do sit down.

Maiden: Thank you daddy

Chief Adjarho: God bless you. How are things generally?

Maiden: I'm fine daddy.

Chief Adjarho: The son of Yusuf the contractor, do you know him?

Maiden: I see him around. Occasionally we greet each other.

Tiro: He says he wants to marry you!

Chief Adjarho: Is that how to discuss a matter Tiro?

Tiro: How else?

Maiden: But I have a fiancée!

Chief Adjarho: We have to discuss that one. I don't approve of that boy Alebai!

Tiro: You have to explain why you do not approve of him!

Chief Adjarho: I don't approve simple!

Tiro: I don't support Yusuf's purchase plan, simple!

Chief Adjarho: Purchase plan?

Tiro: Yes, he wants to use my daughter to purchase your conscience and the right to live freely in this community!

Chief Adjarho: May be I should have allowed you to stay back in Lagos!

Tiro: that wouldn't have changed anything.

Chief Adjarho: Listen, what I say goes in this house!

(Sharp lights out)

Scene Three

(Scene takes place in Dr. Alebai's house. Sparsely furnished in the tradition of the conventional lecturer's standard)

Alebai: Of course Maiden you know I love you. That's the reason I traveled to your hometown to see your dad, to meet your mom and brothers.

Maiden: I know you do. I appreciate your love for me. I love you too. But things are never straightforward in life. If love were all we needed to be together permanently I would have packed all my belongings and moved into your house before the break of dawn. What did the poet say?

> *Wish all we could sing were love songs*
> *I would sing all night to you*
> *Wish love was all we needed to live*
> *I would turn the marketplace into a love store*
> *Wish love was all the pastor could do*
> *I would become a pastor's son*
> *Wish love was all we needed to be together*
> *I would marry you before love is spelt*

Alebai: Moving, very soulful. Most of the poets who wrote about love in the past must have been deep lovers, people who felt rather than think think think all the time!

Maiden: Life was less complicated in their time. There were no Facebook lovers.

Alebai: No Instagram, no Snapchats!

Maiden: You had to express how you felt directly.

Alebai: But the world has changed; even in the churches love for God and man has been replaced with love for money.

Maiden: Yet the pastors continuc to say that love conquers all…

Alebai: Perhaps in the world of the past love conquered all; not anymore.

Maiden: We can only fantasize about love now and what it can do for us…

Alebai: True, my dear, very true. If only love could give us the wings to fly…

Maiden: We would fly into the island of Patmos and dream dreams forever…

Alebai: But the real world is different; dreams are killed midway and we live in limbo…

Maiden: Yes, killed even while we sleep…

Alebai: That's why we have to fight for almost everything. We fight to eat, fight to sleep, fight to love. We even have to fight for life.

Maiden: Last week my father called me for what he called a heart-to-heart talk.

Alebai: Really? What was the subject? Alebai?

Maiden: If he called me to discuss you, for bad or worse I would be happy.

Alebai: I see.

Maiden: He had other things in mind

Alebai: Like what?

Maiden: He told me about a young man who wants to marry me.

Alebai: A young man wants to marry you?

Maiden: Yes. A young man from…

Alebai: Does that still happen? In the 21st century?

Maiden: He said that the young man's father came to see him about the whole thing and that he would like me to be prepared.

Alebai: To be prepared for what?

Maiden: For the whole thing

Alebai: Hmmmmmm! Do you know the man?

Maiden: It's somebody I see around, a guy who wears his father's position in society on his shoulders like an epaulette. We have never gone beyond 'hello' or 'how are you'. Suddenly he wants to marry me.

Alebai: There must be a reason your father is interested in the whole idea.

Maiden: When he told me, I replied that I already have a fiancée. He said that I should perish the thought of ever marrying you.

Alebai: Did he give any reason?

Maiden: He said he will give his reasons later in life and that I should simply respect his wish for now.

Alebai: Later in life?

Maiden: Strange, very strange. I suspect something deeper than what we imagine is going on.

Alebai: Me too. After declaring that he knew my parents and addressing me as his son he turns around to say that we cannot marry.

Maiden: Is it possible they had a quarrel or disagreement that split them before we were born?

Maiden: Possible, very possible.

Alebai: I've never trusted politicians. Now he wants you to marry somebody you hardly know.

Maiden: It's another business deal for him, I think. The man, Alhaji Yusuf happens to be a FLAMES contractor resident in our town.

Alebai: Flames contractor! The almighty Flames of international notoriety.

Maiden: Those blood-sucking bastards who spill oil and make billions.

Alebai: Commerce and marriage! That's it. They both want to use each other. I won't be surprised if the young man is not aware of his father's moves.

Maiden: Well, I will not marry a man just to please my father

Alebai: Good. Can you marry a man and displease your father?

Maiden: I will follow my mind

Alebai: Throughout history, there has always been a marriage between commerce, religion and family. The big families of old arranged marriages between their children to further guarantee their interests. They can be very vicious when their interests are involved. Sadly, it's an old story. I see another 'conqueror mentality' in Yusuf; he wants to cement the relationship between his family and yours, between his business and your community. Against the background of the current upsurge in anti-government, anti-north feelings in your community, he wants to become family with the biggest political family in your home town.

Maiden: What?

Alebai: And you are the channel to that move!

Maiden: I have become a commodity to the father whom I thought loved me

Alebai: Love and money, money and love! Sometimes they are excellent companions. Sometimes we wear one to get the other.

Maiden: Must it always be so?

Alebai: When the British came to the Niger Delta, they promised and then threatened free trade. They initially preached love, exchange of one commodity for another. They later changed the song and made trade compulsory. They dictated the price of commodities. They brought religion and preached love. Some of our leaders at the time were fooled. The ones who were not fooled resisted the British and were soon deposed. Each time I remember what they did to Oba Ovonramwen Nogbaisi, I cry inside my heart. He was removed from his seat in Benin and deported like a criminal to Calabar, away from his people. They gave the same treatment to King Jaja of Opobo. Trade. Commerce. They enslaved people because of money. Now, they have been replaced by local overlords. The same way the British fought and conquered our ancestors so does the State want to conquer our people and take their oil!

Maiden: A repeat of history. And sadly, as insignificant as I am I am caught in the middle of the rift.

Alebai: Your father is both a victim and a beneficiary. He has done his permutations and concluded that he would fly into the heaven of enormous wealth if he could link up with Yusuf, a man from a major ethnic group through marriage.

Maiden: So my happiness does not matter to him

Alebai: I guess he believes that with money all unhappiness would be wiped away. Money is the handkerchief with which the tears of unhappiness are wiped.

Maiden: How wrong are they, how wrong!

Alebai: Very wrong. I had rather remain single all my life than marry a man whom I don't love. The pressure on ladies to get married as sign of social success has driven a lot of young ladies into suicidal marriages.

Maiden: Some friends of mine who married for the sake of marriage are regretting it now. They see it as a sign of failure else that would have opted out of the marriage.

Alebai: Sad. Maiden, I love you. I strayed once and confessed my error to you. I have never strayed again since then. So shall it be all the days of my life.

Maiden: Amen. I've got to leave now. My appointment at the Embassy is for 3pm. If I don't leave now, I will be late.

Alebai: It's okay darling. Should I drive you down?

Maiden: Don't bother darling. I will take the Uber taxi. Relatively cheap and comfortable to do. I know that if you drive into the city, you won't be able to do any other work today.

Alebai: Thanks for being so understanding.

Maiden: You are welcome.

(Sees her off to the door. A kiss and a goodbye. He goes back into the sitting room and sits in front of his computer. His phone rings)

Alebai: Hello!...Yes. No I'm busy at home. Won't be in the office today. ...No...What do you want?...A message? I'm listening...You want to come to the house? Well, if it's that important to you. Bye!

(He is pensive for a while. Then he goes back to the computer. He is on Facebook.)

Alebai: Social media lovers all over the place. I have about four thousand friends on face book. I don't think I have ever met up to one thousand of them in person. But it's the new world, the world of virtual friendship ***(Knock)*** Hello. Who is it?

Voice: It's me.

Alebai: Gberaja?

Voice: Who else? *(He opens the door. She wants to hug him; he avoids her cleverly. A smile on her face. She is seductively dressed)*

Gberaja: My born-again lover, how are you?

Alebai: I'm fine my wayward little friend. How are you doing?

Gberaja: I could be better if you perform your duties!

Alebai: A bottle of coke for you?

Gberaja: No, a small bottle of stout please.

Alebai: Sorry; I don't have Stout in the house.

Gberaja: Is it part of your new resolve? Not to entertain me with alcohol?

Alebai: You little devil, just deliver your message and leave.

Gberaja: So I no longer matter to you *abi*? After what you did to me you want to drop me, just like that?

Alebai: Little girl, what's the message you have?

Gberaja: I still love you

Alebai: I don't love you

Gberaja: You said you loved me once!

Alebai: It was during a moment of passion; a mistake

Gberaja: My love for you will cover for both of us!

Alebai: Impossible.

Gberaja: You said you would protect me!

Alebai: *(Goes back to his computer)* Old story!

Gberaja: It's a new song for me. I still see you in my dreams. The pastor has told me that you are the man for me and that I should be patient.

Alebai: Utter rubbish. Tell your lying pastor to marry you or go to hell!

Gberaja: Abomination!

Alebai: Please yourself.

Gberaja: I will wait. I will wait for you my love, my darling, my daddy. The current wife of our overseer waited for fifty years to marry him because she believed in prophecy. I shall wait for you.

Alebai: And become an old maid!

Gberaja: It doesn't matter as long as it fulfills the will of God!

Alebai: Which God? The god of commerce or the god of lust?

Gberaja: Are you saying you never had any feeling for me? You just used me for one month?

Alebai: It was a moment of weakness. It must not happen again. As you know I have a fiancé; nothing can take me away from her. For your information, she will be returning here anytime. I don't want her to meet you here.

Gberaja: *(Sitting comfortably)* Hmm! You don't want your Number One to meet your Number Two?

Alebai: I have only one woman. That is Maiden!

Gberaja: I intend to wait to see her. We must have this talk today.

Alebai: There is no talk to be had. I have confessed to her how I strayed from the paths of honour. So she knows about you. You have no place in my heart or my house.

Gberaja: I see. I hope you know her father has arranged for a man to marry her.

Alebai: Really? Tell me more!

Gberaja: Yes. The boy is a rich kid. His father is connected to the President of the country.

Alebai: My dear Nigerian BBC, give me more information!

Gberaja: The marriage is fixed for December this year. It's going to be a State wedding. The news has been buzzing in our chat groups with everybody feeling sorry for you Mr. Lover Boy!

Alebai: Are you done?

Gberaja: Done with what?

Alebai: With disseminating false information!

Gberaja: Do not say I didn't warn you.

Alebai: Thanks for your wonderful advice!

Gberaja: You are welcome. So, you see why I must wait for you. I love you; the pastors, not one not two or five have confirmed that you are heaven's choice for me. As a lady of faith, I intend to wait.

(He stands up; opens the door)

Alebai: Thank you. I'm very grateful for the fantastic news which you have brought. You may take your leave now!

Gberaja: I'm not leaving here? You hear? I'm not leaving here. I'm not a piece of rag to be used and dumped. I have cried to my God and He will deal with the matter for me.

Alebai: Out!

Gberaja: *(In tears)* Are you saying I was a mistake in your life?

Alebai: Out!

Gberaja: I will leave. But be sure that if you do not marry me you cannot marry her too!

Alebai: Ouuuuuut! *(She leaves hastily and without the false dignity she had displayed all the while)*

We must avoid quick fixes in life, no matter how tempting they are! I fell for that before; not anymore.

(Sharp lights out)

Scene Four

(Scene takes place in Alhaji Yusuf's office.)

Alhaji Yusuf: *(On the phone)* I have told them. We need to work together and develop the land…no! It is in the interest of everybody…Yes? I know…The adjudicator? Let him disgrace himself in public. We shall settle the matter behind him. ..That one? He is a fool, a big fool. I warned him. I told him not to fight; it's not every time one fights. In business if you can make profit without fighting, it's better…….Now see the trouble he is in!…. When the people begin to gain consciousness after many years of stupor, you must develop new tactics. The prescriptions of yesterday are no longer adequate. …She's fine. Just chopping my money… I don't blame you….Hahahahahahahaha!   Nooo! Cheers. Bye!

Bala: What is the way forward?

Alhaji Yusuf: The way forward? We just go forward *chikena!*

Bala: Just like that father?

Alhaji Yusuf: Yes, just like that. Look here young man. I've found you a wife from a good family.

Bala: A wife, father?

Alhaji Yusuf: Yes a wife! A good one.

Bala: Why?

Alhaji Yusuf: What is why? You want to around producing bastards all over the place?

Bala: No daddy, I don't …

Alhaji Yusuf: Impregnating my house girls!

Bala: But daddy!

Alhaji Yusuf: Sleeping with every little girl employed in the company and squandering money on Brazilian human hair wigs!

Bala: I do not...

Alhaji Yusuf: There's nothing that goes on here that I don't know about.

Bala: I'm sorry daddy.

Alhaji Yusuf: So, you see why you need a good wife to help you settle down and face life squarely?

Bala: I didn't say I was looking for a wife!

Alhaji Yusuf: I know; I am the one looking for a wife for you!

Bala: Okay father!

Alhaji Yusuf: As your father, as a man wise in the ways of the world, I know you are ripe enough to marry!

Bala: But this is all so sudden!

Alhaji Yusuf: Some of the best decisions in life are those that you took without wasting a minute of worry!

Bala: Wife?

Alhaji Yusuf: Your wife-to-be comes from the family of the community leader, Chief Adjarho. He is a man of the people. He is highly respected and anything he says in this town goes!

Bala: I know Chief Adjarho. He is a good man.

Alhaji Yusuf: His daughter takes after him. A no nonsense lady! Loving, firm, beautiful, dependable and intelligent.

Bala: Good to know!

Alhaji Yusuf: You will like her!

Bala: But we have never really met; we've never spoken!

Alhaji Yusuf: You will speak to each other someday!

Bala: After all the years I spent abroad, I would be foolish to marry a girl just because my father wants me to marry her.

Alhaji Yusuf: It's your years abroad that have spoilt you, that have turned you into a bedroom lawyer! Else you wouldn't be arguing with your father!

Bala: I'm not arguing. I just want to understand!

Alhaji Yusuf: You must understand what that can do for our business in these uncertain times. The marriage between the children of the Community leader and the main FLAMES contractor in the country!

Bala: I understand father, yes I do.

Alhaji Yusuf: The ethnic groups in the country should not be fighting. We should intermarry and live together. No man can separate the scrotum from the penis. God has placed all of us in the same geographical zone and we have no choice but to live to**gether.**

Bala: But you should give me time father to think…

Alhaji Yusuf: Think about what? Can't you read between the lines? Can't you read between the lines? See how we are all drifting apart into our small enclaves.

Bala: I know father but…

Alhaji Yusuf: If you really want to sit on the Board of TATAKO International and succeed me when I close my eyes finally you must settle down.

Bala: Yes, I want to settle down. I want to be a husband and father like you.

Alhaji Yusuf: Then follow my path. I shan't mislead you!

Bala: Father, I must respect your wish.

Alhaji Yusuf: Good. You are a good boy!

Bala: However, I have a girl I want to marry. Her name is Amina. Amina has been a member of our family for years. I don't want to disappoint her.

Alhaji Yusuf: Of what value is she? What will she bring into the family?

Bala: But I love her.

Alhaji Yusuf: Listen, young man! You are my heir. I married your mother as a business deal many years ago. Her father was very rich, richer than the State government at the time. At the time I was a struggling young man with prospects, but no money. Her father liked me and gave her to me. He gave me money to start my business. We started. Before long, we produced you. Is she not happy with me? Forget all those sentiments about love.

Bala: So there was no love between you?

Alhaji Yusuf: If there was no love how did we produce you? How have we been able to live together for over thirty years?

Bala: But your time was different. In these days of social media and cable television, we cannot mess with the emotions of people!

Alhaji Yusuf: *Turenchi*!

Bala: She has grown so used to me. God will not forgive me if I…

Alhaji Yusuf: I have not said you should not love her. Love her; you can love her to the moon and back. But she can wait while a local marriage strengthens our business. You are entitled to four wives. So take this one first and follow quickly with the one you love.

Bala: As you know father, how do we handle our religious lives?

Alhaji Yusuf: That is not a problem. Let her practice her faith and you practice yours. Everybody will be happy. You see, the problem with our people is the fact that they take religion too seriously even if they break the rules every day. A Mallam may be drinking beer from his kettle breaking the laws of our religion. But if he sees a man mistakenly tear a page of the Quran, he would be up in arms. What kind of hypocrisy is that?

Bala: What are you driving at father?

Alhaji Yusuf: See what those bastards in the Middle East and North East of Nigeria are doing in the name of Allah. Which Allah?

Bala: That's the question: which Allah?

Alhaji Yusuf: Let us all practice our religion. In the end it the Almighty that will decide who will get what. I have already briefed the girl's father. We shall lead a delegation there next week. Prepare yourself.

Bala: But dad, aren't you moving too fast for me?

Alhaji Yusuf: What time is our Board meeting?

Bala: Twelve noon.

Alhaji Yusuf: We have only ten minutes.

Bala: Yes father!

Alhaji Yusuf: Let us move to the Boardroom!

(They move. In the Boardroom, some people are already seated. Alhaji Yusuf takes his seat)

Secretary: The meeting is hereby called to order!

Alhaji Yusuf: Today's meeting has only one item on the agenda: Integration with host Communities! Any amendments? Are they any additions to the agenda?

Secretary: None!

Alhaji Yusuf: Give us the background

Secretary: This Board meeting has a theme. It is: Making our host Community friendlier to our Business Concern!

Bala: Or making our business friendlier to our host communities!

Alhaji Yusuf: The background!

Secretary: Yes Chairman Sir! In the last five years, the youths of this region have become extremely restive and violent. They complain about all the policies put in place for effective operations. They want more of their people employed in the sector. We recognize the fact that they are often not qualified to hold some of the positions. But perception is important. We must be perceived to taking sides with the local community. Yesterday there protests in the community and they particularly mentioned our company as one of the defaulters.

Alhaji Yusuf: That is the problem. Let us proceed to making suggestions to harmonize relations and help to develop the host community.

Manager: I suggest that we develop short and long term measures.

Alhaji Yusuf: I agree. Any suggestions?

PRO: Let's award scholarships to ten engineering students in the university and promise to employ them when they graduate.

Alhaji Yusuf: Any objections?

Bala: None sir! None Chairman

Alhaji Yusuf: Chief Accountant please work out the financial implications and let me have a figure by midday Wednesday.

Chief Accountant: Yes Sir.

Bala: In that case we will start by making an announcement to the Community leaders that they should submit the names of their sons and daughters who are studying engineering in the university or polytechnic.

Alhaji Yusuf: Such sons and daughters must come from our area of operations; not just anybody.

Bala: I'm almost sure that we can't get up to thirty engineering undergraduates from this town.

PRO: I also suggest that we send about thirty of them to a welding school so they can understand deep water welding.

Alhaji Yusuf: That's an area of weakness in our operations. I will increase the number to fifty. If their boys are fully active in our operations they will be friendlier to us.

PRO: Yes.

Bala: Excellent. We need to develop middle level manpower.

Alhaji Yusuf: I want to employ the Community Leader's daughter as our Community Relations Officer. In fact, the letter of employment is being prepared.

Bala: Chairman, you are moving very fast with your plans.

Alhaji Yusuf: In business we must not waste time once any opportunity for growth offers itself. Manager, I want to sign the letter last thing this evening. I will personally deliver it to Chief Adjarho in the company of the Managing Director.

Bala: As it pleases you chairman.

Alhaji Yusuf: Any other business?

Bala: I move for an adjournment!

Secretary: Seconded!

Alhaji Yusuf: The meeting is declared closed.

(The other members leave the room. Father and son stay back.)

Bala: Are you really serious about going to Chief Adjarho's place this evening?

Alhaji Yusuf: Yes; I'm very serious. *(Calls out)* Manager!

Voice: Coming Sir with the letter.

Alhaji Yusuf: I never joke with my business.

Bala: Do you think it will work?

Alhaji Yusuf: Trust your father!

(Lights out)

Scene Five

(When the scene opens, the three visitors are standing by the door entrance waiting to be ushered in.)

Chief Adjarho: Welcome my party men, and women. Good to see you. To what do I owe this august visit in March?

Chief Awoko: The *Adjerese* himself. Good to meet you at home.

Chief Adjarho: You are always welcome the '*Tebetebe* of Africa

Ms. Oshare: Mi gwo sir

Adjarho: Vre do. Ma vo?

Madam Owhawha: Mi gwo

Adjarho: Vre do. Please be seated. How do I entertain you my visitors?

Madam Owhawha: Kill a goat for pepper soup and *ukodo*!

Adjarho: A goat is too small to receive you. I will slaughter a pregnant elephant!

(Laughter. Benson enters with a tray of drinks and kola nut. Junior comes in too)

Junior: *Mi gwo* sir; *Mi gwo* ma

All: Vre do.

Awoko: How are you?

Junior: I thank God sir. *Adjerese!*

Adjarho: *Onye ese*

Junior: *Udo va wen*?

Awoko: *Tebetebe!*

Junior: *Tebetebe!*

Awoko: *Me tebe yaran*

Junior: *Elizabeti* ..I greet you

Madam Oshare: We greet you too.

Junior: My father says I should welcome all of you. There's kola in the plate. There's money too to prevent the kola from rolling. I am supporting the kola with five hundred naira. That's the message my father sent me.

Awoko: Please receive the kola on our behalf

Junior: Adjerese! Tebetebe says I should greet you. He says that they accept the drink and kola nut. We shall drink together and keep the money. *Sia gware!*

All: **Iy**aaaaa

(Junior takes his leave)

Awoko: What of madam your wife?

Adjarho: She went out. She will return any time from now.

Awoko: Doh! Our elders say *"ame ro to sho ti evwrite'*, water that touches the penis also touches the scrotum! We have come to see you on a special matter.

Adjarho: Hmmm. I'm listening

Owhawha: We plead with you to listen with your two ears *(Kneeling down. Ms. Oshare also kneels down)*

Awoko: *(Clearing his throat)* It has to do with our daughter.

Adjarho: Hope there is no problem?

Awoko: None whatsoever. We have come to beg you about your daughter

Owhawha: She says you do want her to marry the man of her choice.

Awoko: She and her mother believe that if we plead with you would change your mind.

Adjarho: Hmmmmm

Awoko: That is why we are here.

Adjarho: I wish things were as easy as they seem

Owhawha: Is it deeper than what we are hearing?

Adjarho: *(Pensive)* When the hand commits an offence, it is the whole body that gets punished.

Awoko: It's the same white man who created ink that also created an eraser.

Adjarho: A he goat, even inside the pot of stew still smells like a he-goat!

Owhawha: I am lost...

Oshare: Me too. I am lost

Owhawha: We are lost; please come down to our level.

Adjarho: A true father would always be happy when a man steps into the house to say that he wants his daughter's hand in marriage. Why won't I be happy? Will I marry my daughter? God forbid!

All: God forbid!

Awoko: You are not Mr. Crest, that Oyibo-Jekri man who was said to sleep with his pretty daughters!

Oshare: Really? Did he do it?

Owhawha: He did; at least we all believed he did. It was after he died that they got married.

Awoko: No man from this area married them in spite of their beauty!

Adjarho: See how the man ended!

Awoko: In spite of his wealth, he died drinking his piss and eating his shit!

Adjarho: Abomination. That is what happens to a man who behaves like the he-goat and mounts his mother!

Oshare: God forbid. A father and his own biological daughter having sex? What has this world become?

Awoko: When he died, he wasn't buried him in their ancestral home. They buried him in the city so the gods, according to their tradition, would not punish their land.

Adjarho: As I was saying, I have only one daughter; she is my princess and my gold. I love her specially. She went through school without giving me any problem, without always asking for money to buy this or that. In fact, I used to send her money even if she said she wasn't broke because I found out that she was very prudent in handling funds. I look forward to giving her out in marriage. But you see, it has to be a man in whom I have absolute confidence.

Awoko: I know how you feel. I would feel like that too. But this man, what do you have against him? I hear he is a university lecturer. He's much disciplined and although he is not an indigene of our State, he is very close to us. I am told that you knew his parents way back in your younger days. So what is the problem?

Adjarho: Chief Awoko, you know the respect I have for you. But for you I wouldn't be where I am today. I know the support you gave me when I came back home. It is very difficult for me to say no to you. But I am afraid I have to say no.

Owhawha: This is a serious matter. But you haven't told us why you do not approve of Maiden's marriage with her choice?

Adjarho: It is not everything a hunter sees in the forest that he talks about when he returns.

Oshare: Are you saying there is a secret that you don't want us to know about?

Adjarho: When a man comes from another village and begs you to allow him worship your god, you do not ask too many questions.

Awoko: Too many questions would mean prying into deep secrets.

Adjarho: You have hit the nail on the head.

Awoko: When a matter develops pregnancy and its nursing a baby at the same time you must pause for a while to reconsider. So we leave you with one message: we love Maiden. If you can, please allow her to marry her choice.

(They stand up to leave. As they walk to the door, Benson dashes in and says the Bishop is at the door.

***He dashes out again. The trio of political friends
takes their exit and the Bishop comes in)***

Bishop: Peace be unto this house!

Adjarho: Peace be to you too my dear Bishop! You are
welcome to my humble abode. My house will be blessed
today. Please sit down Sir.

Bishop: Thank you my dear Community Chairman. How is
your wife?

Adjarho: She stepped out. I hope she returns in time to
meet you.

Bishop: I hope so too. Chief! My visit will be very short.

Adjarho: Really? But I must receive you in our traditional
way. How many times do you get visited by the Bishop?

Bishop: I ought to make my visits frequently. So pardon me.
Whatever you wish to present please package and send it
to the Bishop's court. It will get to me. I have to be at the
church premises in the next thirty minutes to receive
fellow servants in The Lord who are coming for a crucial
meeting.

Adjarho: As you wish my Lord.

Bishop: Thank you. I will go straight to the point and allow
God to direct your mind. Your wife and your daughter
came to see me last week in connection with Maiden's
choice of husband.

Adjarho: So they came to see you too? A delegation from the community just left here on the same subject!

Bishop: It is because we all hold you and your family in high esteem. I want to plead with you.

Adjarho: You make my heart saying you want to plead with me. Who am I Bishop? I am your humble servant in The Lord's work.

Bishop: Our elders say that when you crown a king even if he is a little boy, you must accord him his due respect. You are the king in this matter. You don't have to give me a reply today. Just think about it. I recognize your right as a responsible father to Maiden. If for spiritual reasons you don't approve of the marriage, I will advise her to listen to you.

Adjarho: If you know the heartache this matter has given me, you would be sorry for me. My wife and Maiden have been unhappy in the house. Anytime I want to eat and the matter comes to my mind, my heart skips a beat. It's that bad. At night I see Maiden crying in her room. It is too much on me. Yet I…

Bishop: It's alright Chief Adjarho. Just pray to God about it and leave the rest to God. I will call you next weekend to find out how things are going. I must leave now. *(Standing up)* God guide and bless you.

(Adjarho sees him off to the door.)

Adjarho: I appreciate this visit. I will get in touch Sir.

Bishop: Bye

Adjarho: Bye my dear Bishop!

(He goes back to his seat crouched in a posture of the defeated, obviously affected by the weight of the pleas.)

Adjarho: What mess have I gotten myself into? God help me. Are you there? The best thing in life is to stay clean and not to do anything that would make you live in secret pain the rest of your life.

Tiro: Chief, I hear you have had a of lot visitors today.

Adjarho: It's true. Thanks to you and your daughter.

Tito: So she is my daughter now!

Adjarho: She is our daughter...

Tiro: That's better…

Adjarho: Except that you both connive to outwit me…

Tiro: What do you mean?

Adjarho: When did you get back?

Tiro: A few minutes ago. How have you been?

Adjarho: Tired, just tired.

(Knock)

Adjarho: Could that be another visitor?

Tiro: Let me find out **(Walking to the entrance)**

Adjarho: Only God knows how many people you have broadcast my family to!

Tiro: It's Alhaji...*(Coming in with Alhaji and his son)*

Adjarho: Alhaji! How are you?

Bala: Good afternoon sir!

Adjarho: Good evening. How are you?

Bala: I'm fine Sir. Mi gwo!

Adjarho: Vre do! *(Laughing)* Who taught you that one?

Bala: I have been in this community long enough to know how to greet my elders in Urhobo! Mi gwo ma!

Tiro: Vre do!

Adjarho: Do sit down!

Alhaji: It's a short visit really. We had a Board Meeting today; and one of our decisions is to reach out more to the community.

Adjarho: That's the true spirit.

Alhaji: We have decided to employ your daughter as Manager Community Relations in our company. We need somebody from this community who understands the business and who can also explain our policies to the people. Here is the letter of employment!

Adjarho: Really? Thank you. People out there may not understand that I didn't lobby you to employ my daughter.

Alhaji: That is the price we pay for being leaders! Too many lies are peddled against leaders. Sadly, the gullible people believe every lie told about their leaders!

Tiro: Thank you Alhaji. I must really thank you though it's our first son, Junior, who is in need of a job right now.

Alhaji: We can always get your son a job in our head office in Lagos. Let me have his CV as soon as possible. We should be able to get him a job in spite of the tight financial times

Adjarho: Two siblings in one company! That wouldn't be too tidy, won't be politically correct in this environment.

Alhaji: It depends on what you want.

Tiro: If you can get him a job in the national oil company that would be great.

Alhaji: Let him send his CV to my office later next week before I travel to Lagos.

Adjarho: That would be a great relief so that he can stand on his own. His CV will reach you; but while you are at it, please get two or three more people employed from other families so they don't attack me.

Alhaji: Consider it done. We must leave now.

Adjarho: Thanks for the visit and the good news.

(They stand up and move to the door. After the good byes husband and wife return to the sitting room)

Tiro: What is going on? Why has Alhaji suddenly become interested in our family?

Adjarho: You should have asked him while he was here!

Tiro: You don't have to answer me that way? Is it part of the pacification agenda, to make us soft and pliable before they take away that which is ours?

Adjarho: I'm just tired of everything. It's been a long an hectic day for me and it's taking its toll on me. I need to take rest awhile before the next emissary of yours comes knocking. They won't kill me with pressure.

Tiro: It's what you sowed. I hope you have taken your medication today.

Adjarho: I don't even remember. Please, get it for me. I don't feel like leaving this seat. The house is spinning.

Tiro: I will get it. Please, take it easy.

Adjarho: Please...*(He slouches on the sofa as Tiro hurriedly leaves the room)*

(Lights out)

Scene Six

(Scene takes place in Mama Alebai's house in Benin)

Abigo Alebai: My dear son, welcome home. How is Lagos?

Alebai: Lagos was fine when I left this morning.

Abigo: It's a bit unusual for you to visit without alerting me. I hope all is well.

Alebai: Yes, all is well. All will be well.

Abigo: I wasn't too surprised though when I saw you because I had already seen your coming in my dream. But in the dream you put on a French suit, dark grey in colour.

Alebai: Mama! Mama the Dreamer! Your dream is correct. Indeed it was when I arrived town that I changed into this caftan!

Abigo: You are welcome. At least tonight I will have company in the house. Your siblings hardly visit with me, although two of them live in town. We only meet in church.

Alebai: That's not nice; I will speak to them about it.

Abigo: Please do it with tact; else they will accuse me after you have gone that I reported them to you.

Alebai: I will handle the situation with tact, trust me.

Abigo: I need to prepare some food for you. Would you like some rice?

Alebai: No mama, I'm fine. I had some food at the restaurant in the bus park before coming home.

Abigo: But that's about four or more hours ago.

Alebai: I don't eat much particularly when it's late.

Abigo: It's okay. I hope you don't think your mother's food is no longer good enough for you?

Alebai: Come on, mother! You know that can't be.

Abigo: Thank God. How was your trip to the Delta the other day? You didn't get back to me.

Alebai: No, I headed straight for Lagos to catch up with lectures the next day.

Abigo: How did it go?

Alebai: That's one of the reasons I am here.

Abigo: Good; let me know my future family-in-laws!

Alebai: You know Maiden; you met her once. That's the girl I want to marry. Her name is Maiden Adjarho.

Abigo: That's an Urhobo name.

Alebai: Yes.

Abigo: The Urhobo are our neighbour; they are descendants of the Bini race. So that's good.

Alebai: Do you know the family?

Abigo: Adjarho is a common name among Urhobo people; so I wouldn't know which of the Adjarhos you are talking about.

Alebai: Mr. Johnson Adjarho!

Abigo: Johnson Adjarho?

Alebai: Yes.

Abigo: The same Johnson Adjarho?

Alebai: He says he knew daddy, that he knew the family some forty years ago; that he knew you when dad worked in a textile mill in Lagos.

Abigo: He must be the same person.

Alebai: Yes, it's the same man!

Abigo: How is he? I haven't heard from him for ages.

Alebai: He is fine.

Abigo: So how did the visit go?

Alebai: Not very well, not very well I am afraid.

Abigo: How?

Alebai: He said I cannot marry his daughter.

Abigo: Did he give a reason?

Alebai: No, he didn't give any reason. He simply said that I cannot marry his daughter and that if you are my mother you should know why.

Abigo: *(Breathes deeply)* There are certain things that are better left unsaid, unknown. The grave covers many secrets!

Alebai: Is there something I ought to know?

Abigo: If he says that you should not marry, so be it. Don't marry her. Look for another girl, please.

Alebai: Mom, what is going on? What went on, what happened in the past that is haunting me now? Am I a bastard child? Was I picked form the road?

Abigo: There are parts of history that should remain dead. If you resurrect them you might kill some people who are alive. It will make some uncomfortable in the grave!

Alebai: But I need to know? I need to know my past, my history.

Abigo: Yes, you will know, when the time comes you will know.

Alebai: Did it have to do with my father?

Abigo: Even if it had to do with your father, no harm can be done anymore. He is gone to rest, no stain on his name. Your father was a perfect gentleman. God bless his soul!

Alebai: Mom, please tell me.

Abigo: I beg you my son in the name of all that you hold dear, do not ask to know what could turn you blind.

Alebai: There is nothing I can't handle. I beg of you!

Abigo: Please let me be. I don't have long to live anymore. Let me live the rest of my days with some dignity.

Alebai: So, it is true mama?

(Silence)

> So it is true?

Abigo: What?

Alebai: Who is my father?

Abigo: Who is your father?

Alebai: Yes, who is my father?

Abigo: *(She is now in tears)* If you know the truth, why are you tormenting me? Odion, why are you tormenting me? I've lived all my years with the hope that our secret would remain so, but alas life has a way of confronting one with the ugly realities of the past.

Alebai: *(In tears too)* What happened? Just let me know the truth.

Abigo: Odion, you have two fathers – one was your father and the other was your daddy; the one who fathered you biologically and the one who looked after you with all diligence throughout his life. Mr. Odion Alebai is your daddy.

Alebai: O my God!

Abigo: I warned you not to dig into the past. The past sometimes has an ugly face. What we do not know about cannot hurt us.

Alebai: But it could lead us into fatal mistakes; it could make us take wrong decisions.

Abigo: It's unfortunate. I am sorry. I am sorry my son. *(She crumbles on the floor. He cannot bear to look at her).* Now I am nothing, nothing to you, nothing to the world.

Alebai: It's not so mama. Are you my mother?

Abigo: Ahhhh! You see? You see why we should not dig too deeply? Do you doubt my motherhood too?

Alebai: I need to know everything; if I have half truths I may make wrong judgments.

Abigo: My son, you are my son. Before I met your father, Johnson was the man I was going to marry. I loved him with all my heart. He loved me too. But my parents objected to the union because we were from different ethnic groups. I begged and begged him; my mother pleaded with him. He firmly objected. This went on for about three years, three years of pain, of uncertainty. And then the man you grew up to know as your father came into the picture, perhaps encouraged by my father. He did all he could to win my heart, from listening to all the insults I hurled at him, rejected his gifts, spurned his advances in anyway. He really did his best to win me. Finally, I agreed to marry him, with Johnson's permission. Yes, Johnson had that hold over me; if he hadn't permitted me I would not have given in.

(Sobbing)

Alebai: So what happened next?

Abigo: The week before our wedding, Johnson and I had a night out; before we knew it, we did it. The condom broke, though I didn't know immediately. It was like a good bye thing. I made up my mind to face my new husband and be faithful to him, which I did. I was never unfaithful to him throughout our marriage. One month after our wedding I found that I had missed my monthly cycle. I could not be sure whether it was your father or Johnson. I couldn't procure an abortion. I kept the pregnancy in the hope that my sin would be covered. I had been warned that I must never procure an abortion…but as you grew up, looking at you, I knew that Johnson was your father. If your father my husband suspected anything, he never said anything about it throughout his life.

Alebai: I don't know what to say.

Abigo: If I had procured an abortion at the time I wouldn't have known you my beautiful son. So I thank God that I didn't act foolishly for the second time.

Alebai: This is too much for one day!

Abigo: That is my story Odion. I beg you to forgive me. My son, I am on the floor, begging God, begging you. I need your forgiveness. I'm crawling to you my son. So you can't bear to look at me? You don't want your eyes to see me groveling in my old age?

Alebai: Stand up mama; don't do this. It's an abomination for you to kneel before me. Please stand up. *(He helps her up without looking into hear teary eyes)* I forgive you; even before I came to ask you I had already forgiven you.

Abigo: Thank you my son! God bless you my son!

Alebai: Thanks for letting me know, for giving birth me, for setting me free. Now I can face the future without looking over my shoulders! Poor Maiden! It's she I feel sorry for the most. As for me I have been misled into committing an abominable act. I also need to ask forgiveness of God Almighty. May God save me!

(Sharp lights out)

Scene *Seven*

(When the scene opens, Dr. Alebai is on the computer banging away. Just as he is about to conclude, he receives a phone call. He answers.)

Dr. Alebai: Hello…I'm fine. How are you? …Good to know. Are you in Lagos? Already? …you didn't tell me my sister. Wanted to catch me unawares? …Your calls? Why shouldn't I take your calls? …it may have been due to poor service by the network provider….Yeah, that's our dear country for you. I'm in the house. Where else do you expect me to be at this time?...Hahahahahaha! That visit? It came out with a pregnant pregnancy. It's not a telephone matter. Oh no! A life-changing experience, my sister. ..Yes, you are my sister…sister in love, sister in Christ! I'm not a mischievous person, you ought to know that by now. I will be expecting you my dear. Cheers!

(Dr. Alebai rises from his seat and faces the audience).

How complicated can this world be some times; how complicated! Wish life was straightforward! Wish we didn't have to run into road blocks and obstacles created before we were born! Certain coincidences are beyond the ordinary…beyond the ordinary. But they could also be revelatory. I still have a lot to learn in life, obviously.

(Knock on the door)

Wait a minute. Who is it?

Voice: Your sister in Christ! *(Opens the door)*

Dr. Alebai: Do come in my beautiful sister in Christ! *(They hug each other. No kissing; Alebai gives her a peck on her forehead)*. You are welcome.

Maiden: How have you been my dear?

Dr. Alebai: I thank God for life! How are you?

Maiden: I am fine, just praying that my dad recovers fully! He is in a bad shape.

Dr. Alebai: I pray for him too, more fervently that you could ever imagine. We need divine intervention.

Maiden: I suspect something is eating him deep inside, something he seems troubled about!

Dr. Alebai: I really don't know.

Maiden: I know from the vacant way he stares into space, saying nothing, a crease in his brow. He gets more uncomfortable each time mom visits and his blood pressure rises.

Dr. Alebai: For real?

Maiden: Yes, for real. It was mom who first noticed and complained. The doctor says that he is troubled by an issue. When mommy asked him he simply looked the other way. I'm shocked how he could have deteriorated so fast within two weeks!

Dr. Alebai: That's man for you; up this minute and down the next!

Maiden: You seem a little bit withdrawn too!

Dr. Alebai: The world has changed since we last met.

Maiden: Don't understand what you mean.

Dr. Alebai: I have undertaken a journey that has changed my life since I visited Benin.

Maiden: I hope we will get the details when the time comes…

Dr. Alebai: The time is soon, or may be now; depends on how we handle things from now.

Maiden: You are being cryptic this afternoon.

Dr. Alebai: The world has not been fair…

Maiden: The world has never been fair…

Dr. Alebai: Maiden, we are blood relations!

Maiden: What do you mean we are blood relations?

Dr. Alebai: Do you remember that during my visit to your hometown your father referred to me as his son?

Maiden: I didn't give it a thought really; I know he did right after you told him who were your parents were.

Dr. Alebai: I thought he did that because he knew my parents!

Maiden: That's what I thought too!

Dr. Alebai: Maiden, we are siblings!

Maiden: Nooooooooooo

Dr. Alebai: shocking, isn't it? After all we have done together!

Maiden: My God! Why? Why? Why?

Dr. Alebai: I don't think God has a role in this matter. It's my mom and our father!

Maiden: For real?

Dr. Alebai: Yes…

(Silence. Maiden is in tears. Dr. Alebai is trying hard to control his tears too)

Maiden: How, what, how are you so so sure?

Dr. Alebai: I visited your dad, well our father in the hospital. Inside the private ward where he was kept, we were alone. When I arrived he was asleep; so I decided to wait; I wanted him to see me that I cared for my future father-in-law. In a short while, he woke up and after a few minutes, he recognized me and said 'my son, how are you? I said I was fine and that I had come to wish him well. He thanked me for not taking things personal and that what he did was in our own interest. I was baffled though I couldn't tell him that it would calm my heart to get to the root of the matter. Suddenly, he breathed deeply and said he was going to speak to me like a man. Here I am going to request you to be calm. This matter must remain between us.

Maiden: Which matter?

Dr. Alebai: What I am going to say to you now. Do you promise never to divulge it?

Maiden: I really don't know; don't know whether I should commit myself without knowing what I am getting into.

Dr. Alebai: Then we should stop the discussion here.

Maiden: Now you are beginning to act like my father!

Dr. Alebai: Perhaps!

Maiden: So?

Dr. Alebai: Promise?

Maiden: I promise.

Dr. Alebai: Good. He said to me: I am your father, your biological father! At least I suspect so. You are going to do a DNA test to confirm our dismiss worries, our concerns.

Maiden: How did that complication arise?

Dr. Alebai: Of course, I asked him. But he said we should run the DNA test first and that a story may not be necessary.

Maiden: Did you?

Dr. Alebai: Of course we did. Fortunately the hospital where he was admitted facilitates for clinic in South Africa. Without disclosing to them what the issues were they took our samples. For two weeks I could not sleep well. I could not...

Maiden: You could not hold any proper conversation on the phone. I wondered what was wrong.

Dr. Alebai: Those were longest and most torturous weeks in my life! What scenario did I not imagine? I made research into different topics, incest, Oedipus complex, family curse, confessions and what have you. Finally the two weeks came. I went to the hospital and the result was ready. It was handed over to me in the presence of father. My hands shook as I opened the envelop. I could see that he was uncomfortable too. It was positive. Johnson Adjarho indeed fathered me.

Maiden: How did it happen? Did he say?

Dr. Alebai: He did, yes did!

Maiden: I feel cold already; very cold; I'm feverish..

Dr. Alebai: At that stage, I didn't know whether to cry or get angry. His eyes remained closed, and I could see tears streaming down his face. He told me the story about how my mom was his lover, how they were to marry, how her parents objected, and how they finally parted ways when your father, Johnson came on the scene. Apparently, they had a last fling and parted ways. Both of them swore never to be unfaithful, never to enter the chambers of adultery; but alas, the damage had been done.

Maiden: It's a difficult question to ask, but if they suspected that the child in the womb could be either my father's or his rival, why did they allow the pregnancy to continue?

Dr. Alebai: Moot question, but I also asked the same question. My mom's answer was that she had been warned against procuring an abortion throughout her life and that if she did she would lose her life. So, here I am; a product of the deadly passion of two irresponsible youths!

Maiden: I don't know what to say.

Dr. Alebai: Don't say anything

Maiden: I need to be specially forgiven for…

Dr. Alebai: You mean we? Yes we need to ask specially forgiveness. But I will not let the past tie me down. I will move ahead in life. We sinned, but it was in ignorance.

Maiden: Ignorance of the law is no excuse…

Dr. Alebai: Yes, in the court of man. But in God's court, we shall be acquitted. I am happy that my father, I mean my dad, Engr. Alebai never found out, or rather he died before the truth came out.

Maiden: My mother, how will she take this. I don't think I want to tell her.

Dr. Alebai: It's left for you to decide whether you want to repeat the kind of mistakes our parents made.

Maiden: How?

Dr. Alebai: The culture of silence, of hiding the past from the present.

Maiden: You think I should tell my mom?

Dr. Alebai: Yes; the final decision will be yours.

Maiden: My father is in a very bad shape. He suffered a massive stroke yesterday.

Dr. Alebai: If he does die, don't tell mommy yet. Perhaps after the funeral, when everything is settled, you may tell her.

Maiden: That makes sense, certainly makes sense. I must leave now

(Silence)

Maiden: I said I must leave now

Dr. Alebai: I heard you.

Maiden: I met you a as a lover; now we are parting ways as brother and sister.

Dr. Alebai: When we meet again, you will be my sister.

Maiden- Our love must remain hanging in the air.

Dr. Alebai: Yes, *Agape* love now!

Maiden: What attracted us to each other? What brought us together? Was it my father I saw in you?

Dr. Alebai: Why did I fall in love with you?

Maiden: Why was I always seeing you in my dreams?

Dr. Alebai: Dreams are not final; they are subject to different interpretations. It may be you wanted me

Maiden: Not a revelation that you are the man for me

Dr. Alebai: The evidence now speaks for itself.

Maiden: What brought us together then.

Dr. Alebai: The sins of our father brought us together; a fatal attraction.

Maiden: There are some secrets that must remain secrets forever, till the end of time. If the truth comes out the world of some people would explode and remain shattered forever.

Dr. Alebai: Yeah!

Maiden: So we shall live in the glass house for the rest of our lives.

Dr. Alebai: I have confronted my mom already; she confessed the truth and begged for forgiveness. I have forgiven her; but I will never tell my siblings the details until she passes away.

Maiden: Life and its contradictions!

Dr. Alebai: My former student, my former lover, my sister good bye. I love you.

(She picks up her bag.)

Maiden: I love you too. Bye

(Hugs. Kisses)

Dr. Alebai: Bye

(She heads for the door; looks back, wipes her tears and steps out into the auditorium. Inside the auditorium Bala is waiting. As soon as they meet, he goes down on his knees, begging her to receive a ring. She refuses; and brings out her letter of employment and shreds it. She leaves him behind. Now alone with a spot light on her, she delivers the final lines)

Maiden: They all want or wanted or loved me for different reasons, some good some not so good. My father loved me because I was his gateway to national wealth, fame and politics. It's sad that my father whom I loved so dearly also commoditized me. Bala wanted me as his wife to in order to establish his father's business in my locality. He has been following me everywhere I go even since the night that they dropped the letter of employment. I will not accept their offer of employment. It's a trap. Let them give it to my brother. I am the oil of love, the one exploited or the one everybody but mom and Odion want to exploit. The only person who truly loved me was castrated by history, even before he was born. my father's fling ensured that. I will go away, I will go my way. I will seek love elsewhere and continue to live my life in full. If people want to make a victim of my beauty and intelligence I do not accept that as my fate. It is a hilly rocky path yet I know that I must find a way. Good bye!

The End

Printed in the United States
By Bookmasters